Montem Primary School
Hornsey Road
London N7 7QT
Tel: 0171 272 6556
Fax: 0171 272 1838

Watching the Weather

Forecasting the Weather

Elizabeth Miles

Heinemann
LIBRARY

www.heinemann.co.uk/library

To order:
☎ Phone 44 (0) 1865 888066
🖹 Send a fax to 44 (0) 1865 314091
💻 Visit the Heinemann Bookshop at www.heinemann.co.uk/library to browse our catalogue and order online.

First published in Great Britain by Heinemann Library, Halley Court, Jordan Hill, Oxford OX2 8EJ, part of Harcourt Education.
Heinemann is a registered trademark of Harcourt Education Ltd.

Editorial: Nancy Dickmann and Daniel Cuttell
Design: Richard Parker and Q2A Solutions
Illustrations: Jeff Edwards
Picture Research: Maria Joannou and Lynda Lines
Production: Camilla Smith

Originated by Ambassador Litho Ltd.
Printed and bound in China by South China Printing Company

ISBN 0 431 19035 6
09 08 07 06 05
10 9 8 7 6 5 4 3 2 1

British Library Cataloguing in Publication Data

Miles, Elizabeth
Forecasting the weather. – (Watching the weather)
551.6'3

A full catalogue record for this book is available from the British Library.

Acknowledgements

The Publishers would like to thank the following for permission to reproduce photographs: Alamy pp. **7** (Robert Harding World Imagery), **24** (The Photo Library Wales); Corbis pp. **13** (Paul Seheult/Eye Ubiquitous), **15**, **17** (Craig Tuttle), **20** (Michael S Yamashita), **26** (Reuters); Digital Vision p. **6**; Harcourt Education Ltd p. **21** (Peter Evans); Masterfile p. **11** (Bill Frymire); NASA pp. **18**, **19**; P A Photos p. **22** (DPA); Reuters pp. **23** (Peter Jones), **27** (David Loh); Rex Features p. **4** (DCY); Robert Harding Picture Library p.**5**; Science Photo Library pp. **8** (British Antarctic Survey), **9** (Phillippe Psaila); Topham Picturepoint pp. **10** (Image Works), **25**; Tudor Photography pp. **28**, **29**.

Cover photograph of a meteorologist attending to the Doppler Weather Radar, reproduced with permission of Corbis/Brownie Harris.

The Publishers would like to thank Daniel Ogden for his assistance in the preparation of this book.

Every effort has been made to contact copyright holders of any material reproduced in this book. Any omissions will be rectified in subsequent printings if notice is given to the Publishers.

The paper used to print this book comes from sustainable resources.

Disclaimer

Contents

Words appearing in the text in bold, **like this,** are explained in the Glossary.

 Find out more about forecasting the weather at www.heinemannexplore.co.uk

What is a weather forecast?

The weather often changes. It might rain or snow. It might feel hot or cold. A weather **forecast** tells us what the weather might be like in the future.

This weather forecast tells us it is going to rain.

Short-term forecasts might tell you what tomorrow's weather will be like. They might also say what the weather will be like for the next few days.

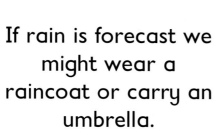

If rain is forecast we might wear a raincoat or carry an umbrella.

Who needs a weather forecast?

The weather affects us all. If hot weather is **forecast**, we can keep cool by putting on light, summer clothes. We might plan a day out in the sunshine.

If a sunny day is forecast, people might choose to go on a picnic.

Fishermen will not go to sea if they know a dangerous storm is on its way.

If cold weather is forecast, we wear thick, warm clothes. If ice is forecast, we might stay indoors to avoid slippery roads.

How do we forecast the weather?

To work out what the weather will be like, we need information from different places. Computers help collect this information.

Weather balloons are released all around the world. They gather information from high in the sky.

Gathering information helps **forecasters** to understand what the weather is like now. This helps them to work out what the weather will be like in the future.

Instruments at **weather stations** gather information, such as the direction of the wind.

Weather maps

Weather maps can show many things, like which way warm and cold air are moving.

Forecasters produce weather **maps** to tell people about the weather. The maps show what the weather is like now or what it will be like in the future.

Some weather maps show lots of information. Other weather maps are simpler and easier for us to understand.

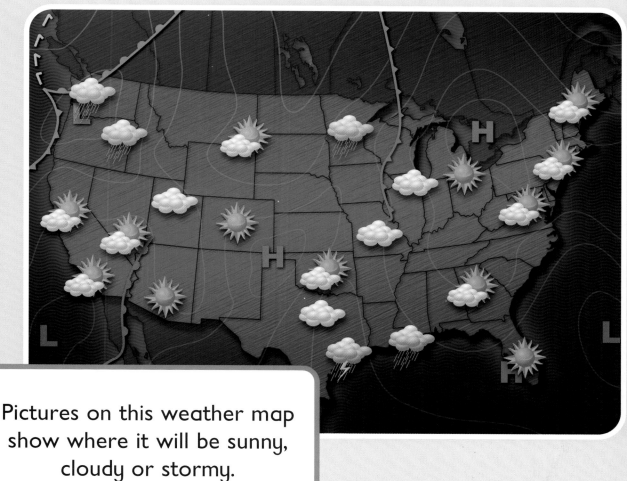

Pictures on this weather map show where it will be sunny, cloudy or stormy.

Air pressure

Meteorologists measure air pressure to help work out what the weather will be like. Air pressure tells us if the air is rising or sinking.

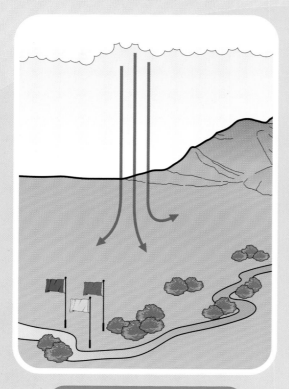

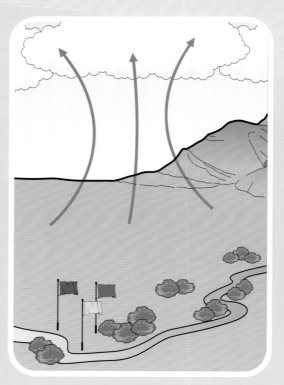

When there is high pressure, the air is sinking.

When there is low pressure, the air is rising.

This barometer shows that the weather will be fair and dry.

Meteorologists use an instrument called a barometer to measure air pressure. Some barometers show what sort of weather we can expect.

Highs and lows

If there is high air pressure coming, **settled** weather is often **forecast**. In summer this often means that the weather will be fine and clear.

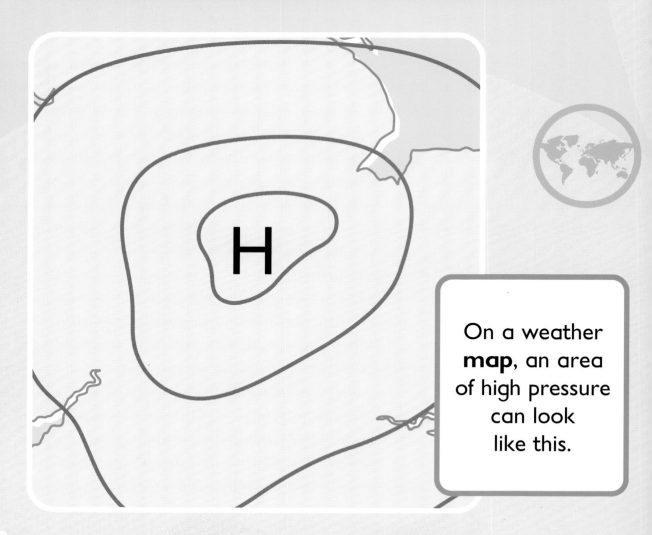

On a weather **map**, an area of high pressure can look like this.

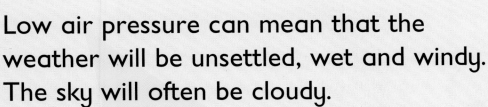

When the air pressure is low it often means rainy and windy weather.

Low air pressure can mean that the weather will be unsettled, wet and windy. The sky will often be cloudy.

Weather fronts

A weather front is where two **masses** of air meet. A warm front is where warm air moves towards colder air. A cold front is cold air moving towards warmer air.

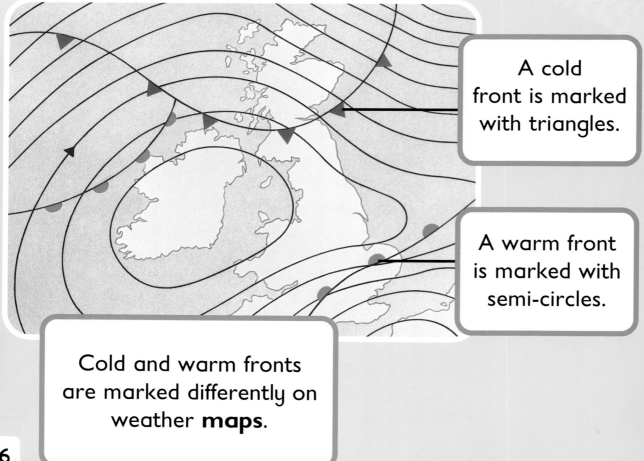

A cold front is marked with triangles.

A warm front is marked with semi-circles.

Cold and warm fronts are marked differently on weather **maps**.

Cirrus clouds can be the first sign of a warm front moving in.

Fronts can bring cloudy, rainy weather. By watching where fronts are going, the weather **forecaster** can tell us where it might rain.

Following a storm

Meteorologists can **forecast** a storm by looking at photographs taken from space. They can see if storm clouds are developing over the sea.

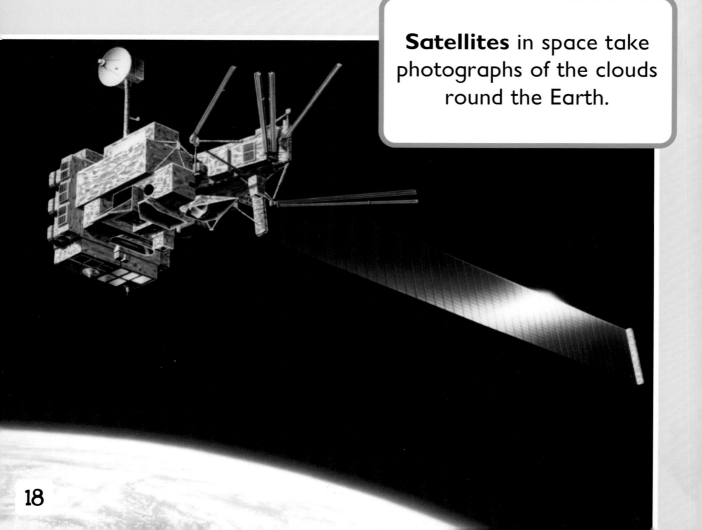

Satellites in space take photographs of the clouds round the Earth.

Satellite photographs show how strong a storm might be. This storm is a **hurricane**.

Meteorologists can measure the wind and work out which way a storm is going. A weather forecast tells people living nearby when the storm might reach them.

Looking at the clouds

Towering black clouds called cumulonimbus can bring thunder and lightning.

We can sometimes **forecast** the local weather ourselves by looking at the clouds. Different kinds of clouds bring different types of weather.

Dark, low-lying clouds bring dull, wet weather.

When low-level clouds begin to cover the sky we know that it might soon begin to rain or snow. Clouds called nimbostratus can bring long periods of rain.

Weather warnings

Forecasters warn people if dangerous weather is on its way. Aircraft flights might have to be cancelled. People might choose to stay indoors if snow or ice is **forecast**.

Snow and ice make roads dangerous. Signs warn drivers to slow down.

Shelters like this help protect people from dangerous storms.

Tornadoes and **hurricanes** can be more dangerous if they come as a surprise. If people are warned they can take **shelter** before the storm arrives.

Animals and plants

Animals and plants need to be kept safe from bad weather. If snow is **forecast**, farmers make sure their animals have food and do not get stuck in **snowdrifts**.

If snow is forecast, sheep may be brought down from the hills, closer to the farm.

Farmers may put special tunnels over their **crops** to protect them from frost.

Frost can kill many plants. Gardeners protect young plants if frosty weather is forecast. To keep the plants warm, they might wrap them in plastic or take them indoors.

Disaster: surprise storm

Weather **forecasts** are not always right. It is difficult to know how strong a storm will be. It is hard to work out where a storm will go, too.

A change of wind direction can bring a surprise storm.

It is hard to warn people that weeks and weeks of dry weather lie ahead.

Long-term forecasts are hard to make. It is difficult to work out how long a type of weather will last.

Project: are they right?

Now you have learnt all about weather **forecasts**, you can check to see how many are right!

You will need:
- white card
- scissors
- coloured felt-tipped pens
- blu-tac

1. On card, draw and colour a simple map of your area.

2. Make coloured card symbols for all the main weather types.

3. For a week, in the morning watch or listen to a local weather forecast. Use your map to record what they say the weather will be like that day. Stick the right symbols on your map.

4. Each day, compare the weather outside with your weather map.

5. Were the weather forecasts right?

Glossary

crop plants grown for food or to sell, such as vegetables and fruit

forecast try to work out what the weather will be like in the future

forecaster person who works out and tells you what the weather might be like

frost frozen water vapour close to the ground

hurricane storm with very strong winds and heavy rain

map drawing of all or part of the Earth

masses large areas of air

meteorologist person who studies the weather

satellite spacecraft that goes round the Earth and carries equipment like cameras

settled dry weather that stays the same for some time

shelter strong building, specially built to stay up in very strong winds

snowdrift thick snow that is piled up by the wind

tornado storm with winds that spin very fast

weather balloon balloon that carries weather instruments high into the sky

weather station building where air, wind and cloud measurements are taken and recorded

Find out more

More books to read

Measuring the Weather: Forecasting Weather, Alan Rodgers and Angela Streluk (Heinemann Library, 2002)

Nature's Patterns: Weather Patterns, Monica Hughes (Heinemann Library, 2004)

What Makes it Rain?, Susan Mayes (Usborne, 2001)

Websites to visit

http://www.bbc.co.uk/weather/weatherwise
A website packed with information about how the weather affects us, weather images and facts, and lots of fun games, projects and activities.

http://www.onlineweather.com
Find out and see what the weather is like all around the world.

Index

Titles in the *Watching the Weather* series include:

Watching the Weather — Clouds	**Watching the Weather — Dew and Frost**	**Watching the Weather — Rain**
Hardback　　　0 431 19022 4	Hardback　　　0 431 19023 2	Hardback　　　0 431 19024 0
Watching the Weather — Sunshine	**Watching the Weather — Thunder and Lightning**	**Watching the Weather — Forecasting the Weather**
Hardback　　　0 431 19025 9	Hardback　　　0 431 19026 7	Hardback　　　0 431 19035 6
Watching the Weather — Snow	**Watching the Weather — Wind**	**Watching the Weather — Fog and Mist**
Hardback　　　0 431 19036 4	Hardback　　　0 431 19037 2	Hardback　　　0 431 19034 8

Find out about the other titles in this series on our website www.heinemann.co.uk/library